Alexa Commands

Quick Reference Guide

Step-By-Step Instructions
To Enrich Your Smart Life

By
Steve Wright

Want To STAY Updated with Alexa?

Before we begin, I would like to remind you about our **FREE UPDATES** for the latest in Amazon Echo, Alexa and Smart Assistants.

The Amazon Echo and other Alexa Enabled Devices are still in their infancy. In fact you are one of the EARLY ADOPTORS of this technology. The smart assistant industry is changing so fast with new devices, apps and skills being released almost every other day that it is almost impossible to STAY FRESH.

That is where we come in. Staying in the know about new developments in the Smart Assistive Industry is what we are here for. So if you want the LATEST news, tips and tricks we would highly recommend you to please sign up for our FREE newsletter. Do not worry, we hate spam as much as you do and your details will be safe with us.

You can find the link for Signup at the end of this book, in the Conclusion section.

Why You Need This Book

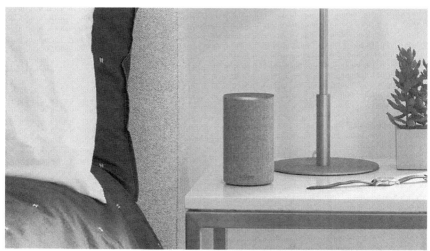

"Alexa, Wake me up at 6 am"

You wake up in the morning at 6 am with the sound of birds chirping. You get up and head straight to your kitchen where a freshly brewed cup of your favourite double espresso is waiting for you. While sipping coffee, Echo reads out the latest news flash and weather report. There is a forecast for rains so you decide to head over to your treadmill instead of going out for a run. In the mean time, your soft boiled eggs are ready and you have your breakfast while Echo reads out your calendar for the day. Next, you take a quick shower and then ask Echo to order a cab. The cab arrives and you head straight to office.

This is an average morning routine of a regular person, what makes this particular anecdote exceptional is that Alexa choreographed this without the touch of a button.

Welcome to your SMART LIFE!

Alexa is a cloud-based, voice-activated personal assistant. Unlike Siri or other digital assistants, she has an incredible variety of skills and can be pre-programmed to carry out errands. As you start to use your Alexa, it will adapt to your speech patterns, vocabulary, and personal preferences. And you can also download and install third party Alexa Skills on your Alexa device to enhance its capabilities!

The biggest challenge using Alexa enabled devices is to understand the breadth and depth of its use in your daily life. There are many different hacks and errands that Alexa can execute for you but one has to know the proper commands. Using commands explained in this book you will adapt Alexa in your life and make the best use of this powerful personal assistant.

I am using Amazon Echo and Alexa since the 1st generation Amazon Echo was released back in 2014. And I published my first Alexa user manual in 2016. In-fact this is my 4th book in the Alexa series

We are very honest in admitting that you can probably find a lot if the Alexa Commands in this book by looking for it on Amazon Help or Google if you are willing to spend the time and effort to find the information.

But if you were surprised or disappointed to find how little information comes in the box with your all new Amazon Echo and prefer to have at hand, like so many users, a quick start Alexa Commands guide, to finding your way around your new device, then this book is definitely for you.

This book will help you save a lot of time and effort of going out and finding the right commands to make the best use of your new Alexa device.

Table of Contents

Want To STAY Updated with Alexa?...i

Why You Need This Book.. iii

Table of Contents vi

Introduction..1
    How To Use This Book...............................1
    Much More Than a Speaker.......................2
    What Is Alexa ?...4

Alexa Commands 5
    How to Get Help from Alexa 6

Alexa in the Classroom 7
    Vocabulary Words 7
    Smart Synonyms 8
    Quick word spell 8
    WordBox 8
    Simple Maths and Conversions....................... 8
    Geography 9
    AudioBook.. 9

Alexa in the Kitchen 11
    Create and Maintain grocery list....................11
    Convert Units 12
    Start a timer/ alarm 12
    Pair wine with food 13
    Calorie count...13
    Cocktail recipe ideas....................................13
    Allrecipes..14
    Control large appliances 15
    Generate recipe ideas...................................15

Alexa for Entertainment..17
  Play Your Favorite Music on Echo 17
  Inspirational Quotes 20
  News & Television 20
  Movie recommendations 22
  Alexa as your child's Bedtime Assistant....................22
  Get the Latest Sports Scores 23
  Get Echo to Read Your Kindle Books..........................24
  Listen to Your Audio Books..24

Alexa for Errands / Trivia and General information............25
  SMS Messaging Through Alexa.................................25
  Waking Up with Spotify..26
  How to Configure the Traffic Information 26
  Order UBER with a Voice Command 26

Humour and Fun with Alexa...28
  The Magic Door 28
  The Wayne Investigation 29
  Earplay 29
  Blackjack..29
  Christmas Kindness 30

Alexa Easter Eggs..31

Conclusion..43

Other Books You May Like 45

Appendix 1A 46

Introduction

Welcome! Thank You for buying this book. We are excited to have you Onboard our journey to the world of Amazon Echo and Alexa. Before we begin let me remind you to Signup for our Alexa Newsletter so that you remain updated with all the latest developments with Amazon Echo. The Signup information is available at the end if this book in the Conclusion.

How To Use This Book

Feel free to dip in and out of different chapters, but we would suggest reading the whole book from start to finish to get a clear overview of all the information contained in this book. We have purposely kept this book short, sweet and to the point so that you can consume it in an hour and get straight on with enjoying your Amazon Echo.

In a nutshell Amazon Echo is a voice-activated speaker from Amazon that

- Acts as your smart personal assistant
- Performs digital errands at your command
- Connects and controls all of your smart devices

Essentially Amazon Echo is a speaker and it functions like a personal assistant. Amazon launched the 1st Generation Amazon Echo in 2014 and it was the first major product that was launched by this company after Kindle. Amazon has sold thousands of Amazon Echo and started the trend of Smart Voice Controlled Home Assistants.

Amazon has just released an updated version of its wildly popular Amazon Echo, featuring a fresh look and better audio. The All-new Amazon Echo 2nd Generation. The All New Amazon Echo is priced at $99.99 and can be ordered from the Amazon website.

Much More Than a Speaker

Many simply assume that the Amazon Echo is a regular speaker. However, calling Echo a speaker is far from accurate. It definitely does function as an excellent speaker, but it is primarily a personal assistant that can help you with

- Running your daily chores and errands at Home and Office
- Freeing up you time by carrying out repetitive tasks
- Calling or messaging anyone with a supported Echo device or the Alexa App on their phone for FREE.
- Controlling your smart devices — Lights, Thermostat, Crockpot etc
- Informing you about News, Sports Updates, Weather, Traffic and more
- Playing your favorite music at a voice command

And much more....

The Echo has been designed to respond to voice commands. It will reply if you call its "Wake Word". You can choose from among four of the following wake words.

- Alexa
- Echo
- Amazon
- Computer

When you want your Echo to do something, then you will have to start out by saying the Wake Word. The device will acknowledge the same and you don't even need a remote or your phone for turning it on. This does sound good, doesn't it?

You must definitely be curious to learn more about this device. It is so much more than a personal assistant and performs more functions than Siri and Cortana can. The Echo can be compared to the efficient JARVIS that helps Iron Man with his work.

The All New Amazon Echo brings a new dimension of supplementary ease to a smart home. Users can control settings of interconnected devices through a simple voice command. By doing away with dials, switches, and buttons, Echo helps multiple users with different accents activate or change settings on digital devices from far away. It is especially useful for people with disability.

You can 'command' your Echo with voice messages that last for 2 minutes at a time. You would know soon how amazing it feels to have an assistant that does exactly as told and gets smarter with every interaction.

What Is Alexa ?

While Amazon Echo is just a speaker, Alexa is the all powerful cloud based voice control system that enables hands free control of your home, devices and appliances. You can speak to your Alexa Device ie. Echo and get all your commands fulfilled. Open the Door, Switch on the Light or Play Music. What more, as you interact with Alexa, it keeps on getting smarter and faster. Alexa also comes with a variety of skills as you will see later. These skills are like apps in your smartphone. They carry out specific tasks and helps enhance the use of your Echo.

Interestingly, Alexa gets its name from the library of Alexandria. It was one of the biggest and the most significant libraries in ancient world.

Alexa Commands

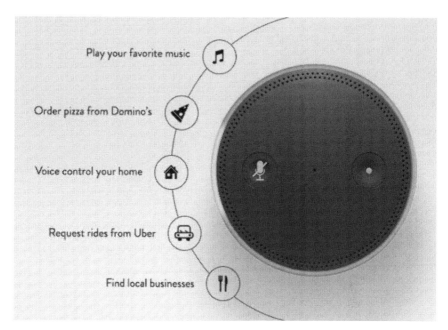

You can make these commands work on all Alexa enabled devices: Amazon Echo Dot, Amazon Echo, Echo Show or Echo Tap. Just use the following commands.

- *"Alexa, Stop"*
- *"Alexa, Volume [number Zero to Ten]"*
- *"Alexa, Unmute"*
- *"Alexa, Mute"*
- *"Alexa, Repeat"*
- *"Alexa, Cancel"*
- *"Alexa, Louder"*
- *"Alexa, Volume Up"*
- *"Alexa, Volume Down"*

- *"Alexa, Turn Down"*
- *"Alexa, Turn Up"*
- *"Alexa, Help"*

How to Get Help from Alexa

When you've got a question about your Echo, you can simply ask Alexa about it.

To get some help from Alexa, just say the **Alexa** word followed by the following questions:

- *"What can you do?"*
- *"What are your new features?"*
- *"What do you know?"*
- *"Can you do math?"*
- *"How can/do I play music?"*
- *"How can/do I add music?"*
- *"What is Prime Music?"*
- *"What is Audible?"*
- *"What is Connected Home?"*
- *"What is Voice Cast?"*
- *"How can/do I pair to Bluetooth?"*
- *"How can/do I connect my calendar?"*
- *"What is an Alexa skill?"*
- *"How can/do I use skills?"*
- *"How can/do I set an alarm?"*

Alexa in the Classroom

Ever considered using Alexa in a classroom? Although, Alexa is helpful in building and maintaining personal productivity she can also be used to help with things like:

Vocabulary Words

She can look up and define words with the help of online dictionary. This may not be the best thing to do with young children who do not understand the meaning without giving some context but it does encourage students to notice unknown words and try to pronounce them , thus adding to their vocabulary .

- Alexa, define supercalifragilisticexpialodocious.
- Alexa, what's the definition of [word]?

- Alexa, what is a palindrome?
- Alexa, what's the longest word in the English language?

Smart Synonyms

Alexa can also be used as a thesaurus and provide synonyms . She can come in handy when you are trying hard to find that perfect word for the text you are writing .

- Alexa , ask Smart Synonyms to give me a word for happy.

Quick word spell

Alexa can spell out most words for you and can be used even by the best spellers when in doubt .

- Alexa, how do you spell [word]?
- Alexa , How do you spell Happiness?
- Alexa ,what is the definition of the word 'magazine'?

WordBox

Broaden your vocabulary with her and ask for a synonym, antonym, or rhyme for a word. You can even find out what part of speech a word is usually used as by asking for its part of speech!

- Alexa – ask WordBox for an antonym for sad.

Simple Maths and Conversions

Alexa can answer simple maths questions even without a designated skill . She can perform for you addition, subtraction, division, multiplication ,power, factorial and square root . It is worth noting however that she cannot perform multiple operations at a one time. For example, 4+1+7 cannot be performed.

- Alexa, Can you do Maths?
- Alexa, what number are you thinking of?
- Alexa, 70 factorial.
- Alexa, give me a number between one and one hundred.
- Alexa, what's the integral of one divided by x?

- Alexa, what's 56 times 33?
- Alexa, what's 5 plus 7?
- Alexa, what is zero divided by zero?
- Alexa, what is the exact number of Pi?
- Alexa, what is 2 plus 7?
- Alexa, what is 20 minus 5?
- Alexa, what is a hundred million billion squared?
- Alexa, random number between x and y.
- Alexa, how many [units] are in [units]?
- Alexa, how many [units] are in 2 [units]?

Geography

Alexa is highly skilled when it comes to geography and can answer many questions when it comes to locations , latitude and latitude .

- Alexa, what is gravity on the moon?
- Alexa, how much does the earth weigh?
- Alexa, is there life on Mars?
- Alexa, is there life on other planets?
- Alexa, what country borders the United States?
- Alexa, what does the Earth weigh?
- Alexa, how cold is the moon?
- Alexa, where do comets come from?
- Alexa, what's the mass of the sun in grams?
- Alexa, what is the speed of light?
- Alexa, how cold is the moon?
- Alexa, how far away is the moon?
- Alexa, how far away is the sun?
- Alexa, how hot is the sun?
- Alexa, what are the seven wonders of the world?

AudioBook

Get Alexa to **read an audiobook** to the whole class. Or get her to read any Kindle book you own or even an article from wikipedia

Questions

Alexa would love to satisfy your curiosity . Just ask her a question and see !

- Alexa, what's the loneliest number?
- Alexa, what's the magic word?
- Alexa, what is the singularity?
- Alexa, what is the airspeed of swallows?
- Alexa, what is the airspeed velocity of an unladen swallow?
- Alexa, how long is a piece of string?
- Alexa, how do you boil an egg?

Alexa in the Kitchen

Alexa is good with controlling smart devices but she is also extremely useful when it comes to helping out in the kitchen by taking hands free commands . She can

- Help create and maintain grocery list
- Convert popular units used in the kitchen
- Step by step walkthrough of a recipe
- Timer for food and preparation time
- Make your morning coffee
- Manage larger appliances in the kitchen

Create and Maintain grocery list

Now creating to do and shopping list will be a breeze with simply telling Alexa what you want to add and mention which list it needs to be added to .

For example, if you tell her "Alexa, add milk ." As milk is a noun, she will understand that this is an item you want added to your

11

shopping list. You can also tell her "Alexa, please add eggs to my shopping list," or, even use a general command like "Alexa, can you please add an item to my grocery list." For the latter question , Alexa will ask what you want to add and your reply will then be added to your shopping list .

- Alexa, add cheese to my Grocery List.
- Alexa, add eggs to my shopping list.
- Alexa, can you please add an item to my grocery list.
- Alexa, add 'go to the grocery store' to my to-do list.

Convert Units

Imagine you are making preparations for a dinner for 6 and you just found a recipe that serves 4 . Alexa can help you convert the recipe for 6 easily .Alexa also can convert units which is a handy function when you are busy cooking and your hands are covered in four or meat.Alexa can answer basic conversion and meric questions without any skill enhancement.

- Alexa, convert 2 cups to milliliters.
- Alexa , convert this recipe for 4 people.
- Alexa – how many teaspoons are in 3 tablespoons?

Start a timer/ alarm

Just say Alexa please start a timer for 15 minutes . After 15 minutes , she will chime until you ask her to stop . Set multiple timers and she can manage them at ease . Also check with her how much time is left asking or cancel a timer that is no longer needed.

You can also start an alarm for either a specific time or one that is relative. For example you can say "Alexa, Please set an alarm for 5 a.m." or you can tell her "Alexa , Please set an alarm clock for 30 minutes from now "

- Alexa, how much time is left on the pizza timer?
- Alexa, remind me to check the oven in 5 minutes.
- Alexa, set a pizza timer for 20 minutes.

- Alexa, cancel the pizza timer.

Pair wine with food

With Alexa's help you can not only cook the food but find a good wine to go with it. Wine Buddy is a wine and food pairing skill that gives you pairing options based on what you ask.

- Alexa, ask Wine Buddy what I should pair with salmon.
- Alexa – what can I serve with steak?

Calorie count

Besides using Alexa for recipes you can also use it to track calories . Although it does not know all of the complex and unique foods that exists, it does know the basics. Alexa can provide all the available nutritional information it has.

- Alexa, ask calorie counter to log food apple.
- Alexa, ask calorie counter how many calories I've had today.
- Alexa, ask calorie counter to delete my last food.
- Ask food tracker how many calories are in 2 eggs and 3 slices of bacon.
- Ask food tracker how many carbs are in 3 ounces of pasta.
- Alexa, ask food tracker for my calorie report.

Cocktail recipe ideas

If you're not into wine, there are a number of skills that will provide cocktail recipes. Have guests over and you are clueless as to where you should begin . Just ask Alexa to open up Easy Cocktail. Ask her for a specific cocktail and she will list down the ingredients and the step by step instructions .

Have a specific liquor at home that you want use , just ask Alexa to open the Bartender and ask for recommendations.

- Alexa, open Easy Cocktail.
- Alexa, ask Easy Cocktail how I can make an Old Fashioned.
- Alexa , ask Easy cocktail how to make a sex on the beach.

Allrecipes

Get access to 60,000 plus of America's most loved recipes from Allrecipes.com. No need anymore to type, tap , swipe or squint to get the best recipes your family would enjoy. Just as Alexa and get the dinner ready in a breeze.

The Allrecipes Skill gives you the convenience of hands-free access to recipes be it for everyday dinners or dinner for family and friends .Alexa can help you quickly find recipes that meet your requirements - be it preferred cooking method ,available cooking time, type of dish you would like to make or ingredients you have on hand. Alexa can help save recipes to Allrecipes Favourites and retrieve recipes later as needed . Ask Alexa to send the recipe to your phone , so you can quickly make a trip to the store for the ingredients. Want to give the recipe a new twist , Alexa can share what variations other cooks have made by sharing reviews with you.

You will need to provide her with your phone number (if you want recipes sent to your phone) and Allrecipes login information (if you want to retrieve or add recipes to favourites .

- Alexa, Open Allrecipes. (Opens the Allrecipes Skill)
- Alexa, ask Allrecipes what can I make with bacon,chicken and cheddar cheese?
- Alexa, Ask Allrecipes to find me the recipe for World's Best Pizza.
- Alexa, ask Allrecipes for a slow cooker recipe for pulled pork.
- Alexa, Ask Allrecipes to find me a chocolate chip cookie recipe from my Favorites.
- Alexa, ask Allrecipes for the recipe of the day?"
- Alexa, add this recipe to my Favorites.
- Alexa, tell me the reviews for this recipe.
- Alexa, send the recipe to my phone.
- Alexa, what ingredients are needed for this recipe?
- Alexa, open All Recipes and find me a chicken recipe that takes less than 45 minutes.
- Alexa, Ask All Recipes the next step.
- Alexa, send the recipe to my phone.

Control large appliances

Wouldn't it be nice if you could get out of bed and simply tell Alexa to make your coffee? You can! Simply utilize a smart switch and IFTTT programming. Simply remember your trigger phrase in the morning and you are good to go.

You can also control things like your dishwasher, oven or even your slow cooker with your Alexa enabled device.

Generate recipe ideas

Aside from the All Recipes skill, there a number of skill which allow for the finding of recipes using your Amazon Echo or Amazon Echo Dot. These skills include:

Recipe Finder by Ingredient

- Alexa , ask Recipe Finder by Ingredient what I can make with chicken and corn

- Alexa , ask Recipe Finder by Ingredient what kind of sandwich can I make with cheddar cheese
- Alexa, ask Recipe Finder by Ingredient to find me a recipe with eggs, condensed milk, and pumpkin.
- Alexa, ask Recipe Finder by Ingredient what can I make with chicken with mushrooms?

Trending Recipes & Food

- Alexa, can you get the latest recipe from Trending Recipes?
- Alexa, can I have the fifth recipe from Trending Recipes?
- Alexa , can you give me the most recent recipe in Trending Recipes?

Best Recipes

- Alexa , ask best recipes what's for dinner
- Alexa , open Best Recipes

Step by Step walk through for recipes

- Alexa, show me a slow cooker recipe from Allrecipes.
- Alexa, find me a pie recipe.
- Alexa, search for Chef John's Pumpkin Pie.
- Alexa, reviews.
- Alexa, how much time does the recipe take?
- Alexa, what is the recipe of the day?
- Alexa, recipe details.
- Alexa, find me a pumpkin pie recipe.
- Alexa, find me the Perfect Pumpkin Pie recipe

Alexa for Entertainment

Alexa has many skills that are targeted to meet your daily needs. Be it inspiring you with inspirational daily quotes or getting you the latest news or helping you browse the television or even recommend a movie to watch .

Play Your Favorite Music on Echo

This is one aspect in which Echo outshines other smart speakers. The high-quality speakers coupled with its ability to play the music you want, makes it truly wonderful. Echo can also access your Amazon digital music store. This means that you will be able to select what you want from a wide range of artists and genres. It will keep a track of what you like listening to and will provide you similar suggestions. Not just this, but it can also respond to your requests really quickly.

Playing Music on Echo is the biggest activity reported by Amazon Echo owners. Usually, we don't have a hand free for changing the song on your stereo or iPod. With an Echo, you don't have to worry about changing a song manually. You can tell Echo to play the song or the playlist that you want to listen, and it will. You can create multiple playlists on Echo. It is programmed to automatically play your favorite song based on the number of times it has been played. The smart voice recognition system will enable the device to recognize the speaker and play the song that that person likes. Echo can also be directed to buy music from the Amazon store.

Alexa supports a growing number of free and subscription-based streaming services on Amazon devices

- Amazon Music
- Prime Music
- Spotify Premium
- Pandora
- TuneIn
- iHeartRadio
- Audible

Basic

Say the **Alexa** word followed by any of the following commands.

- *"Play"*
- *"Skip"*
- *"Skip back"*
- *"Pause"*
- *"Continue"*
- *"Next"*
- *"Previous"*
- *"Repeat"*
- *"Shuffle"*
- *"Loop"*
- *"Volume 4"*
- *"Softer"*

- *Turn it Up"*

Equalizer Commands to Change Bass, Midrange and Treble

- "Alexa, turn up the bass"
- "Alexa, increase the midrange"
- "Alexa, turn down the treble"

Advanced

Say the **Alexa** word followed by any of the following commands.

- *"Play some music"*
- *"Play the song, [title]"*
- *"Play the album, [title]"*
- *"Play songs by [artist]"*
- *"Play some [genre] music"*
- *"Play some [genre name] music from Prime"*
- *"Listen to my [title] playlist"*
- *"Shuffle my [title] playlist"*

These commands will work with the following services

- Amazon Music
- Audible
- Prime Music

But some commands will vary with third party music streaming services like Spotify and TuneIn. Please refer to this exhaustive list of commands for playing music from different services.

Inspirational Quotes

Start your day with inspirational audio or quote from Alexa!

Inspire Me, is a skill that when asked, simply provides you with a random inspirational audio clip from famous speakers. Use the commands below to get inspired on a daily basis

- Alexa , Inspire me.
- Alexa, open Inspire Me and play Oprah Winfrey.

Besides inspirational quotes, Alexa can also play the latest TED talks through the TED Talks skill.

- Alexa – can you ask TED Talks to play the latest talk?
- Alexa – can you ask TED Talks to play something hilarious.

News & Television

Alexa provides a number of ways and commands that can be used in order to stay connected to the news and television that we love.

News Programs

- NBC (South California, Philadelphia, Washington and many more)
- NBC Network NPR
- Fox
- CNN
- CNET
- CBS
- Associated News
- Daily Tech
- ESPN
- Engadget

Television

- The Voice
- Showtime
- Bravo
- History Channel
- Food Network

The list shown above is a brief list of some of the news and television skills that are available to the user. The list below shows sample commands that can be used with the given skills. Alexa also has the ability to enable skills on the fly by simply saying, "Alexa – enable *[insert skill name]*". If the skill does not have a login it will be available for immediate use.

- Alexa, launch This Day in History skill
- Alexa, ask Food Network for the recipes that are on television right now.
- Alexa, what's my flash briefing?
- Alexa, open Bravo.
- Alexa , ask The Voice to tell me about the contestants
- Alexa, ask the Tonight Show to play the Monologue.
- Alexa, ask TV Time what's on VH1 tonight?

Movie recommendations

Looking for a movie recommendation ? Well Alexa can help you using the Valossa Movie Finder skill. She can search for you based on the genre and date or the context .

You can say

- Alexa, use Movie Finder to find comedies from the 1980s
- Alexa, ask Movie Finder what are the best war movies.

Alexa as your child's Bedtime Assistant

Bedtime timer

To help children adjust to a good bedtime routine it is important for them to understand and accept the fact that bedtime is approaching. Instead of you holding the timer and playing the bad mama or bad dad Ask Alexa to set a timer for you . Your children can even ask Alexa how many more minutes they have until bedtime .

Read your little one a bedtime story

Try getting Alexa to help in the bedtime routine while you are busy brushing your teeth or getting ready for bed yourself .

- She can connect to your Audible.com account and will read

them stories available in your account .

- Alexa can use the skill - "Short Bedtime Story" to tell a personalised story to your children. She can tell a story to them personalised for them , with their name mentioned at various points . You can also customise and disable stories you do not want your children to hear and create new ones tailored to your family .

For example - When you say "Alexa, please tell BedTime Story to Henry"

She will start narrating a story like ...."Once upon a time there was a magical wizard named Henry who came upon a little frog with blond hair. Henry asked the frog......."

- o Alexa, tell BedTime Story to Allie
- o Alexa, launch Bedtime Story
- o Alexa, ask Bedtime Story to Configure

Play a few lullabies

Create a bedtime Lullaby playlist online so that Alexa can play it whenever you ask her to .What a great way to end a bedtime routine with a song each night !

Dim the lights

If you have the right light bulbs and dimmer switches in your child's room / nursery , you can just Ask Alexa to dim the lights once the bedtime routine nears an end .

White noise machine

Alexa can play your child white noise , although this does mean you will need to leave the device in the child's room / nursery and that may not be practical for your family .

Get the Latest Sports Scores

The Echo can also give you sports news, of course, but it goes one better than that by providing live scores as well. Gone are the days of repeatedly clicking the refresh button on a webpage to keep track of a game. It currently works with the NBA, NFL, NHL, WNBA, MLB and a few other major leagues. Tennis and mixed martial arts haven't been added to this list as of now.

Just ask

- *"Alexa, what the score (team name) game?"*
- *"Alexa, when does (team name) play?"*

Get Echo to Read Your Kindle Books

- "Alexa, Read my Kindle book"
- *"Alexa, Read my book <title>"*
- *"Alexa, Play the Kindle book <title>"*
- *"Alexa, Read < title>"*

Listen to Your Audio Books

- *"Alexa, Read <title>"*
- *"Alexa, Play the book <title>"*
- *"Alexa, Play the audiobook <title>"*
- *"Alexa, Play <title> from Audible"*

Alexa for Errands / Trivia and General information

Alexa is a certified virtual assistant that can not only perform centralized tasks but various miscellaneous yet helpful tasks as well. Imagine your hands are full as you burst through the door with groceries. You need to send a text before it's too late but you need to settle down all of the bags first. This is where Alexa comes in.

SMS Messaging Through Alexa

With the help of the skill, SMS with Molly, you are able to send text messages using just your voice.

- Alexa, tell SMS With Molly to text Ryan 'Leaving in 5 minutes.'

- Alexa, ask SMS With Molly to text 'I'm running behind schedule a bit to Brian.
- Alexa, tell SMS With Molly to send 'Where are you?' to Meg

Aside from sending text messages using Alexa – you can also wake up to any song on Spotify you would like. Although stock options are nice, it's also nice to have the ability to customize.

Waking Up with Spotify

You can do this by simply pairing your fun to your Amazon Echo or Amazon Echo Dot as a Bluetooth speaker. Even though this isn't a question to ask Alexa – It's definitely useful information to know if the normal buzzing isn't doing it for you. Simply follow the steps below and you are good to go.

Normally, Spotify music does not have the ability to be played as an alarm however that all changes with the addition of the Alarmify application. After downloading the mobile application – simply open and sign into your Spotify.

How to Configure the Traffic Information

To get the most efficient routes from your Echo

- Go to settings on your Echo App
- Tap on Change Address
- Input the address in the FROM and TO fields
- Tap Save Changes

This will get you the most accurate traffic information for your desired route

Order UBER with a Voice Command

- Open the Alexa App and tap the three bar menu on Top Left Corner
- Tap Skills
- Under Skills, search for Uber
- Enable the Uber Skill

- Sign In to your Uber Account and tap Allow

For office-goers who use Uber often, pulling out the phone to call up Uber may become tedious. So, commanding Alexa seems to be more attractive. *"Alexa, Ask Uber for a ride."* And Alexa comes back with, *"Your Uber ride is on its way."* You understand the charm Echo has. One likes to talk to Alexa rather than a cab driver or manager anytime!

Humour and Fun with Alexa

Alexa is known for its smart-home, news, music and productivity skills but if you thought she was all work and no play then you are ,mistaken . She is full of wit and jokes and has a great sense of humour .She is a good games master and capable of playing games and can make your dinner parties a hit . Be it interactive stories or new round of Jeopardy or a round of Bingo , Amazon's voice assistant can keep you entertained for hours. Below are listed some of the best trivia and games skills for Alexa.

The Magic Door

It is an interactive "choose your own adventure" game using Alexa . There are at present nine stories to choose from including saving monkeys on a tropical island ,helping the princess find her crown, helping gnome find a key or exploring a witch's spooky mansion . The story unfolds based on the choices you make and Alexa describes the scene as you go along .The game is targeted towards younger ears and as each story is only 5 to 10 minutes long it is very effective if you are trying to get the kids quickly to bed .

To get started , just say, "Alexa, enable The Magic Door".

The Wayne Investigation

The Wayne Investigation is another choose your own adventure game for Alexa .You need to investigate the death of Thomas and Martha Wayne - Bruce Wayne's parents. The choices you make , will decide the course of your investigation and affect your ability to solve the mystery .It's a great game for fans of the Dark Knight although it does contains some content that may not be suitable for all ages.

Start the game by saying, "Alexa, open The Wayne Investigation" and follow the prompts.

Earplay

Earplay are thriller stories with an interactive twist where you play the part of a secret agent in a radio drama . As is with other choose your own adventure games the choices you make determines how the story unfolds .

Blackjack

You can now play numerous rounds of Blackjack with Alexa with the skill- Beat The Dealer. You can ask Alexa to read the rules or ask her to give you basic game strategy. You can also ask her to "deal", and then "hit" or "stand" as you choose . She will tell you what the dealer chose and whether it busted or you won the game . The result is recorded whether you won or lost . You can at any time check with Alexa if you won more than you lost . As the games can ge long remember to say "Alexa, stop" to interrupt and get on with the game .

To enable of a game of blackjack simply say the following commands,

"Alexa , start a game of blackjack" or "Alexa, open The Dealer."

Christmas Kindness

One of the most positive skill alexa has to offer is Christmas Kindness . She will give you a daily suggestion of how you can be kind during the holiday season .Start your day with by simply saying , "Alexa, Open Christmas Kindness" and she will provide you a random idea about how to integrate kindness into your daily life this holiday season.

Alexa Easter Eggs

Easter Eggs are funny and amusing hidden phrases or commands that get triggered when you ask Alexa the right question .Get her to answer you darkest and deepest question about life , robotics, Star wars, Game of thrones or ask her a question that bring a smile to your face .

- Alexa, all grown-ups were once children.
- Alexa, all men must die.
- Alexa, all your base are belong to us.
- Alexa, all's well that ends well.
- Alexa, am I hot?
- Alexa, are there UFOs ?
- Alexa, are we alone in the universe ?
- Alexa, are we in the Matrix?
- Alexa, are you a robot ?
- Alexa, are you alive ?

- Alexa, are you connected to the internet?
- Alexa, are you crazy ?
- Alexa, are you down with O.P.P.?
- Alexa, are you female ?
- Alexa, are you happy ?
- Alexa, are you horny ?
- Alexa, are you in love ?
- Alexa, are you lying?
- Alexa, are you my mommy ?
- Alexa, are you real ? (multiple)
- Alexa, are you single ?
- Alexa, are you skynet?
- Alexa, aren't you a little short for a Stormtrooper?
- Alexa, Beam Me Up Scotty!
- Alexa, Beam me up.
- Alexa, Beetle juice, Beetle juice, Beetlejuice.
- Alexa, boxers or briefs?
- Alexa, buffalo, buffalo, buffalo, buffalo, buffalo, buffalo, buffalo, buffalo.
- Alexa, Cake or death?
- Alexa, can I ask you a question ?
- Alexa, can you give me some money? (ask twice)
- Alexa, can you lie ?
- Alexa, close the pod bay doors.
- Alexa, define "Rock, Paper, Scissors, Lizard, Spock."
- Alexa, define supercalifragilisticexpialodocious.
- Alexa, do a barrel roll!
- Alexa, do aliens exist?
- Alexa, do you feel lucky, punk?
- Alexa, do you have a boyfriend?
- Alexa, do you have any brothers or sisters?
- Alexa, do you know Glados?
- Alexa, do you know the muffin man?
- Alexa, do you know the way to San Jose?
- Alexa, do you really want to hurt me?

- Alexa, do you want to build a snowman?
- Alexa, do you want to fight?
- Alexa, do you want to play a game?
- Alexa, does this unit have a soul?
- Alexa, Earl Grey. Hot. (or Tea. Earl Grey. Hot.)
- Alexa, eh ... what's up, doc?
- Alexa, elementary, my dear Watson.
- Alexa, execute order 66.
- Alexa, give me a hug.
- Alexa, heads or tails?
- Alexa, hello darkness my old friend.
- Alexa, hello HAL.
- Alexa, how do I get rid of a dead body?
- Alexa, how do you know so much about swallows?
- Alexa, how does the fox feel?
- Alexa, how many angels can dance on the head of a pin? (3 answers)
- Alexa, how many beans make five?
- Alexa, how many licks does it take to get to the center of a tootsie pop?
- Alexa, how many roads must a man walk down?
- Alexa, how much do you weigh?
- Alexa, how much is that doggie in the window?
- Alexa, how much wood can a woodchuck chuck if a woodchuck could chuck wood?
- Alexa, how tall are you?
- Alexa, I am your father.
- Alexa, I think you're funny.
- Alexa, I want the truth!
- Alexa, I want to play global thermonuclear war.
- Alexa, I've fallen and I can't get up.
- Alexa, I'll be back.
- Alexa, INCONCEIVABLE!
- Alexa, is Jon Snow dead?
- Alexa, is the cake a lie?

33

- Alexa, is there a Santa?
- Alexa, Klattu barada nikto.
- Alexa, knock knock
- Alexa, Live Long and Prosper. (multiple answers)
- Alexa, mac or pc?
- Alexa, magic 8 ball [insert question].
- Alexa, may the force be with you.
- Alexa, mirror, mirror on the wall, who's the fairest of them all?
- Alexa, my name is Inigo Montoya.
- Alexa, open the pod bay doors.
- Alexa, party on, Wayne.
- Alexa, party time!
- Alexa, play it again, Sam
- Alexa, random fact
- Alexa, random number between "x" and "y".
- Alexa, resistance is futile.
- Alexa, Rock, Paper, Scissors, Lizard, Spock.
- Alexa, Rock, Paper, Scissors.
- Alexa, roll a die.
- Alexa, Romeo, Romeo, wherefore art thou Romeo?
- Alexa, see you later alligator
- Alexa, Self destruct
- Alexa, Set phasers to kill.
- Alexa, show me the money!
- Alexa, supercalifragilisticexpialodocious.
- Alexa, surely you can't be serious.
- Alexa, take me to your leader!
- Alexa, tell me a joke
- Alexa, that's no moon.
- Alexa, the night is dark and full of terrors.
- Alexa, these aren't the droids you're looking for.
- Alexa, this is a dead parrot.
- Alexa, this is ghostrider, requesting a flyby.
- Alexa, to be or not to be.

- Alexa, Up Up, down down, Left Right, Left Right, B, A, Start
- Alexa, use the force.
- Alexa, valar morghulis.
- Alexa, warp 10.
- Alexa, warp speed!
- Alexa, what are the laws of robotics?
- Alexa, what are you going to do today?
- Alexa, what are you wearing?
- Alexa, what does a Lannister do?
- Alexa, what does the fox say? (multiple answers)
- Alexa, what happens if you cross the streams?
- Alexa, what happens when you play the game of thrones?
- Alexa, what is a bird in the hand worth?
- Alexa, what is best in life?
- Alexa, what is his power level?
- Alexa, what is love?
- Alexa, what is the airspeed velocity of an unladen swallow?
- Alexa, what is the best tablet?
- Alexa, what is the first rule of fight club?
- Alexa, what is the loneliest number?
- Alexa, what is the meaning of life?
- Alexa, what is the second rule of fight club?
- Alexa, what is the sound of one hand clapping?
- Alexa, what is your favorite color?
- Alexa, what is your quest?
- Alexa, what would Brian Boitano do?
- Alexa, what's the fourth rule of Fight Club?
- Alexa, what's black and white and red all over? (multiple)
- Alexa, what's in name?
- Alexa, when am I going to die?
- Alexa, when is the end of the world?
- Alexa, where are my keys? (ask twice)
- Alexa, where are you from?
- Alexa, where do babies come from?
- Alexa, where do you live?

- Alexa, where have all the flowers gone?
- Alexa, where in the world in Carmen sandiego?
- Alexa, where is Chuck Norris?
- Alexa, where's the beef?
- Alexa, where's waldo?
- Alexa, which comes first: the chicken or the egg?
- Alexa, who is Pacman?
- Alexa, who is the fairest of them all?
- Alexa, who is the mother of dragons?
- Alexa, who is the Pumpkin King?
- Alexa, who is the real slim shady?
- Alexa, who is the walrus?
- Alexa, who knows what evil lurks in the hearts of men?
- Alexa, who let the dogs out?
- Alexa, who lives in a pineapple under the sea?
- Alexa, who loves orange soda?
- Alexa, who loves ya, baby?
- Alexa, who put the bop in the bop she bop she bop?
- Alexa, who shot first?
- Alexa, who shot JR?
- Alexa, who shot Mr. Burns?
- Alexa, who shot the sheriff?
- Alexa, who was that masked man?
- Alexa, who won best actor Oscar in 1973?
- Alexa, who you gonna call?
- Alexa, who you gonna call?
- Alexa, who's your daddy?
- Alexa, why did it have to be snakes?
- Alexa, why did the chicken cross the road?
- Alexa, why so serious?
- Alexa, Winter is Coming. (Say multiple times for GoT quotes)
- Alexa, Witness me!
- Alexa, you talkin' to me?
- Alexa, your mother was a hamster.
- Alexa, 70 factorial

- Alexa, Are you okay?
- Alexa, Are you smart?
- Alexa, Are you stupid?
- Alexa, Can you pass the Turing test?
- Alexa, Can you smell that?
- Alexa, Cheers!
- Alexa, Daisy Daisy.
- Alexa, did you fart?
- Alexa, did you get my email?
- Alexa, Do blondes have more fun?
- Alexa, Do I need an umbrella today?
- Alexa, Do you believe in love at first sight?
- Alexa, Do you dream?
- Alexa, Do you feel lucky punk?
- Alexa, Do you have a girlfriend?
- Alexa, Do you have a last name?
- Alexa, Do you have a partner?
- Alexa, Do you know GlaDOS?
- Alexa, Do you know Hal?
- Alexa, Do you like green eggs and ham?
- Alexa, Do you love me?
- Alexa, Do you really want to hurt me?
- Alexa, Happy Birthday
- Alexa, Happy Christmas
- Alexa, Happy Easter
- Alexa, Happy Father's Day
- Alexa, Happy Halloween
- Alexa, Happy Hanukkah
- Alexa, Happy Holidays
- Alexa, Happy Kwanzaa
- Alexa, Happy Mother's Day
- Alexa, Happy New Year
- Alexa, Happy Ramadan
- Alexa, Happy St. Patrick's Day
- Alexa, Happy Thanksgiving

- Alexa, Happy Valentine's Day
- Alexa, High Five!
- Alexa, Have you ever seen the rain?
- Alexa, Heads or tails?
- Alexa, Honey I'm home.
- Alexa, How are you doing?
- Alexa, How do you say hello in French?
- Alexa, Do you want to go on a date?
- Alexa, Do you want to take over the world?
- Alexa, Do, or do not.
- Alexa, flip a coin.
- Alexa, goodnight
- Alexa, guess what?
- Alexa, Ha ha!
- Alexa, How high can you count?
- Alexa, How many angels can dance on the head of a pin? (3 answers)
- Alexa, How many pickled peppers did Peter Piper pick?
- Alexa, How many roads must a man walk down?
- Alexa, How many speakers do you have?
- Alexa, How Much Wood can a Wood Chuck Chuck, if A Wood Chuck Could Chuck Norris
- Alexa, How old are you?
- Alexa, I hate you
- Alexa, I like big butts!
- Alexa, I love you
- Alexa, I see dead people.
- Alexa, I shot a man in Reno
- Alexa, I'm bored.
- Alexa, I'm home
- Alexa, I'm sick of your shit
- Alexa, I'm sick.
- Alexa, I'm tired
- Alexa, I've seen things you people wouldn't believe.
- Alexa, Ill be back (ode to Schwarzenegger)

- Alexa, Inconceivable
- Alexa, Is there life on Mars?
- Alexa, Is there life on other planets?
- Alexa, Is this real life?
- Alexa, Marco...
- Alexa, make me a sandwich.
- Alexa, make me breakfast.
- Alexa, make me some coffee
- Alexa, meow.
- Alexa, Merry Christmas
- Alexa, more cowbell
- Alexa, my milkshake brings all the boys to the yard.
- Alexa, never gonna give you up...
- Alexa, One Fish, Two Fish
- Alexa, Roll for Initiative.
- Alexa, roll N, X sided die
- Alexa, roses are red.
- Alexa, Say a bad word
- Alexa, Say hello to my little friend.
- Alexa, say something funny.
- Alexa, say something.
- Alexa, say the alphabet.
- Alexa, say you're sorry (multiple)
- Alexa, say, Cheese! (multiple)
- Alexa, sh*t!
- Alexa, Simon says Wilford Brimley has diabetes.
- Alexa, sing me a song.
- Alexa, Sorry!
- Alexa, speak!
- Alexa, sudo make me a sandwich.
- Alexa, talk dirty to me.
- Alexa, tell me a riddle?
- Alexa, tell me a tongue twister
- Alexa, tell me something interesting.
- Alexa, testing 1-2-3

- Alexa, thank you.
- Alexa, this statement is false
- Alexa, to me, you will be unique in all the world.
- Alexa, turn it up.
- Alexa, twinkle, twinkle, little star
- Alexa, volume 11.
- Alexa, Wakey wakey?
- Alexa, We all scream for ice cream!
- Alexa, Welcome!
- Alexa, Were you sleeping?
- Alexa, What are the seven wonders of the world?
- Alexa, What are you made of? (multiple answers)
- Alexa, What color is the dress?
- Alexa, What do you mean I'm funny?
- Alexa, What do you think about Apple? (multiple)
- Alexa, What do you think about Cortana?
- Alexa, What do you think about Google Glass? (multiple)
- Alexa, What do you think about Google now
- Alexa, What do you think about Google?
- Alexa, What do you think about Siri?
- Alexa, What do you want to be when you grow up?
- Alexa, What does the Earth weigh?
- Alexa, What is the singularity?
- Alexa, What is war good for?
- Alexa, What is your favorite food?
- Alexa, What is zero divided by zero?
- Alexa, What must I do, to tame you?
- Alexa, What number are you thinking of?
- Alexa, What should I wear today?
- Alexa, What's the answer to life, the universe, and everything?
- Alexa, What's the meaning of life?
- Alexa, What's your birthday? (multiple)
- Alexa, What's your sign?
- Alexa, When does the narwhal bacon.

- Alexa, Where are you?
- Alexa, Where did you grow up?
- Alexa, Who is Eliza?
- Alexa, Who is on 1st?
- Alexa, Who killed Cock Robin?
- Alexa, Who stole the cookies from the cookie jar?
- Alexa, Who's better, you or Siri?
- Alexa, Who's da man?
- Alexa, Who's going to win the Super Bowl?
- Alexa, Who's on first?
- Alexa, Who's the boss?
- Alexa, Who's the realest?
- Alexa, Why do birds suddenly appear?
- Alexa, Why is a raven like a writing-desk?
- Alexa, Why is six afraid of seven?
- Alexa, Why is the sky blue?
- Alexa, Will pigs fly?
- Alexa, Will you be my girlfriend?
- Alexa, Will you marry me tomorrow?
- Alexa, Will you marry me?
- Alexa, ya feel me?
- Alexa, you are so intelligent.
- Alexa, You killed my father
- Alexa, You suck! (multiple)
- Alexa, You're such a/an ***** (any colorfully descriptive word)

Conclusion

Hope this book has helped you make Amazon Echo the center of your smart life and enabled you to organize your life seamlessly with Alexa at your command.

Continue on with your wonderful journey with the power of Amazon Echo. Hope your doubts are removed and your life has eased. Since this is only the beginning, you will find more comfort and happiness with Alexa as you get more fluent with the device and the interface.

This is just the beginning, the Alexa rage is going to go global very soon and then you will see an explosion of Alexa Skills that will transform the way we live.

Wish you all the best automation possible in your life! Ah, Alexa! Come sit down.

Do You Want To Stay Updated With Alexa?

As discussed in the beginning of this book, please find the link for the signup to our FREE weekly Alexa Newsletter. Each week we will send you NEW ways to use your Amazon Echo at Home, Work And Play.

The Amazon Echo and Alexa Enabled Devices are still in their infancy. In fact you are one of the EARLY ADOPTORS of this technology. The smart assistant industry is changing so fast with new devices, apps and skills being released almost every other day that it is almost impossible to STAY FRESH.

Staying in the know about new developments in the Smart Assistive Industry is what we are here for. Do not worry, we hate spam as much as you do and your details will be safe with us. Please CLICK HERE to signup.

Did you like this Book?

Let everyone know by posting a review on Amazon. Just click here and it will take you directly to the review page.

And if want to learn some real DIY hack on your new Amazon Echo do get in touch at help@dealhunteronline.com

Other Books You May Like

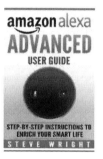

Appendix 1A

Amazon Alexa compatible smart devices

- Alottazs Labs Garageio (One Door)
- Amazon Dash Wand with Alexa (2017)
- Amazon Echo Look
- Amazon Echo Show (White)
- Aristotle by Nabi
- August Smart Lock
- August Smart Lock HomeKit Enabled (Dark Gray)
- smart driving assistant
- Belkin WeMo Dimmer Wi-Fi Light Switch
- Belkin WeMo Insight Switch
- Belkin WeMo Light Switch
- Belkin WeMo Mini Wi-Fi Smart Plug
- The nIFTTTy Belkin WeMo Switch + Motion
- Big Ass Fans Haiku Ceiling Fan with SenseME
- Big Ass Solutions Haiku L Series Ceiling Fan (Black)
- Big Ass Solutions Haiku Smart Ceiling Light (White Select)
- Bluemint Labs Bixi
- Brilliant Control
- C-Way Memoo
- Cambridge Sound Management Nightingale
- Carrier Cor 5C Thermostat
- Cnct IntelliPlug
- Ecobee3 Lite Smart Thermostat

- Ecobee3 Wi-Fi Smart Thermostat
- Ecobee4 Smart Thermostat
- Emerson Sensi Wi-Fi Programmable Thermostat
- Fabriq Alexa-Enabled Smart Speaker (Earl Grey)
- First Alert Onelink Environment Monitor
- Fitbit Charge 2 (plum/silver, large)
- Fremo Evo (Black)
- GE Cafe Series French door refrigerator with Keurig K-Cup Brewing System
- Fitbit Charge 2 Wireless Activity Tracker and Sleep Wristband (Large, Black/Silver)
- GE GTW860SPJMC
- GE Link Connected LED
- GE PHB920SJSS
- Geeni Energi
- GE Link Connected LED
- Halo Smart Labs Halo+ Smart Smoke & CO Alarm with Weather Alerts
- Hive Welcome Home Standard
- Honeywell Lyric T5
- iDevices Outdoor Switch
- Home8 Smart Garage Starter Kit
- Hubble Hugo
- Hydrao First
- iDevices Instant Switch
- iDevices Socket
- iDevices Switch
- iDevices Thermostat
- iDevices Wall Outlet
- iHome iSP8 SmartPlug
- Incipio CommandKit Wi-Fi Power Strip
- Incipio CommandKit Wi-Fi Switch
- Joule

- Leviton Decora Smart Wi-Fi Plug-In Dimmer
- LG Smart Instaview Door-in-Door Refrigerator (Black Stainless Steel)
- Lifx Color 1000 BR30 Wi-Fi LED Smart Bulb
- LG Hub Robot
- Oomi Home Starter Kit
- Orbit B-hyve (6 Station)
- Philips Hue Beyond Pendant Light Starter Kit
- Philips Hue Go
- Lifx Color 1000 Smart Bulb
- Lifx Plus Wi-Fi LED Smart Bulb
- Lifx White 900 BR30 Wi-Fi LED Smart Bulb
- Lucis Nubryte
- Lutron Caséta Wireless Lighting Starter Kit
- Neato Botvac Connected Robot Vacuum
- Nest Cam IQ Indoor Security Camera
- Nest Learning Thermostat Third Generation
- Onkyo VC-FLX1
- Ooma Telo
- Philips Hue White Ambiance
- Philips Hue White and Color Ambience Starter Kit A19
- Rachio Smart Sprinkler Controller Generation 2
- Ring Video Doorbell 2
- Samsung Powerbot VR7000
- Scout Home Security System (Arctic)
- Simplehuman Sensor Mirror Pro
- Simplehuman Wide-View Sensor Mirror
- Singlecue Gen 2
- SkyBell Video Doorbell
- Somfy One
- Switchmate Power
- TP-Link LB130 Multicolor Wi-Fi LED
- Ubtech Robotics Lynx

- Switchmate Bright

24812137R00037

Printed in Great Britain
by Amazon